EXPLORE

The World of DOGS

Joan Blackmore

DERRYDALE BOOKS
New York

A SALAMANDER BOOK

First published by Salamander Books Ltd.,
129-137 York Way, London N7 9LG,
United Kingdom.

© Salamander Books Ltd. 1991

ISBN 0-517-05909-6

8 7 6 5 4 3 2 1

This 1991 edition published by Derrydale Books, distributed by
Outlet Book Company, Inc., 225 Park Avenue South,
New York, New York 10003.

Printed and bound in Belgium.

CREDITS

Designed and edited by: The Book Creation Company

American consultant: Hal Sundstrom

Artwork by: John Francis and John Green

Color separation by: P & W Graphics, Pte. Ltd., Singapore

Printed by: Proost International Book Production, Turnhout,
Belgium

CONTENTS

THE WORLD OF DOGS

◀ **The Labrador is widely regarded as one of the best all-round dogs in the world, and can adapt happily to a variety of different types of work.**

▲ **Dog and man have been partners for many centuries.**

Becoming a dog owner is a very important step. Every year people buy dogs without thinking carefully about the type of dog which is best for them, and the needs of the breed they have chosen. This is especially true if you are considering buying a guarding or working dog, because many of these breeds need firm training from puppyhood. This easy-to-use book aims to help you pick the right dog for you and your family, and to understand what your dog needs so that it will be healthy, happy and obedient.

So, use the information in the following pages to help you find a new and faithful friend.

The History Of Dogs

Thousands of years ago dogs lived and worked with people. They helped cavemen to hunt animals and they guarded settlements. The dogs were rewarded with food and the warmth of the fireside. Over the centuries these dogs developed in different ways.

About a hundred years ago dog owners began to organize dog shows. Then Kennel Clubs were set up in many countries. These clubs set down official standards for each breed, and now breeders try to produce dogs that look as much like these 'correct' examples as possible.

The Dog Family

The dog's most ancient ancestor was an animal called miacis which lived about 40 million years ago. Miacis was a small creature with short legs, a long back and a long head. Ten groups of dogs developed from this early ancestor:

Cape Hunting Dog – has large, upright ears, uneven spotted markings.
Maned Wolf – has long legs, large, erect ears, a mane of long black hair.
Wolf – the closest relative of the dog. It is grey and hunts in a pack.
Hyena – hyenas are very fierce and have a strange, laughing cry.

South American Bush Dog – a powerful dog with a strong head and small ears.
Dhole – has a reddish-brown coat with a long body and short legs. It is a ferocious pack dog.
Jackal – a small dog that hunts at night in a pack.
Racoon Dog – has rings round its eyes and is yellow, black or grey with stripes. It hunts in a pack at night.
Coyote – looks like a small wolf with a long body and tail. It hunts alone or in pairs.
Fox – has a reddish coat and a bushy tail. It hunts alone, usually at night.

▶ **The wolf is the closest relative of the dog. This is a Timber Wolf which lives in the forests of northern Asia, Europe and North America.**

▼ **The hunting dog of East Africa is a very efficient hunter and competes with man for food. It is almost extinct.**

CHOOSING A DOG

▲ Many dogs are kept in unhealthy and dangerous conditions. Even small and medium sized dogs need somewhere to play in safety.

◄ Large dogs like Rottweilers need proper training from puppyhood if they are to develop into good pets.

Choosing a dog is a difficult task and needs a great deal of thought. To help you make your decision, we have drawn up a list of questions that you need to ask yourself.

The Right Dog For You
● Do you live in a house or flat? Is it large or small?
● Do you have a garden? What size is it? Is it well fenced in?
● What will the dog cost to buy, inoculate and feed?
● Are you prepared to spend time every day exercising, training and grooming your dog?
● Who will be at home with your pet during the day when you are at school and unable to look after it?
● Who will look after your dog when you and your family are away on holiday?
● Does an elderly person live with your family, or do you have very young sisters or brothers?

Your answers will help you decide whether a dog is right for you. Your dog needs care and attention, and it is important that you have the time to spend looking after your pet.

Selecting a breed is also important. The breed section on page 16 will help you choose.

▲ Pure-bred dogs with a pedigree can be very expensive to buy. Cross-breeds (above) are usually full of character and make very good pets.

▶ There are dogs for all types of people and each one is super for someone. Remember this old saying: 'There is only one perfect dog in the world and everyone has it!'

Finding Your Dog

Where to look for your dog depends on whether you want a pure-bred or cross-bred. A pure-bred has parents of the same breed. If you want a pure-bred with a pedigree, you will have to visit a breeder. A pedigree means that the dog's ancestors are known. A cross-bred, or mongrel dog has mixed parentage.

Try to visit more than one breeder. Always ask to see the puppy's mother - this should be possible and will give you a good idea of what your pup should develop into. If the mother is shy or nervous the chances are that her pup will be the same.

Watch and handle the puppies. Do not take the bossiest pup or the smallest. Check that the eyes are bright and the ears are clean and not smelly. Look for skin problems such as rashes.

Ask the breeder what health problems the breed suffers from. You should be shown official documents proving that the pup's parents do not have these problems. Inoculation as well as worming records should also be provided along with a diet and feeding schedule.

You can find a mongrel by looking at advertisements in your local newspaper or visiting humane society animal shelters.

LOOKING AFTER YOUR DOG

▲ There are many kinds of dog food available. This selection shows fresh, dry, moist and tinned food, as well as mixer biscuits.

◄ A good diet will keep your dog healthy and strong.

Food is the dog's most basic requirement . A puppy requires different feeding from an adult dog. If your dog is to be strong and healthy, you must make sure that you give him the right amount of food. At eight weeks of age a puppy will need four small meals every day. The breeder will give you a diet sheet which tells you the type of food your puppy should be given.

At three months the puppy should have three meals each day, at six months two larger meals and at one year one large meal each day.

You may like to give your dog fresh, raw beef bones to chew. These keep the teeth clean and your dog happy.

Never give your dog sweet foods or food that has gone bad. Be selective, especially when giving titbits.

Grooming
All dogs need to be groomed. Grooming takes dust, dirt and tangles out of the coat. It is good for the dog's skin and most dogs enjoy it.

A wire-pin brush will remove dead hairs and a

▶ **Long-haired dogs need regular grooming to keep their coats free of tangles.**

metal dog comb can be used to remove tangles and to clean the brush. Do not use a stiff, harsh brush on a thin-skinned dog with a short coat. As you groom, look out for fleas, lice and ticks.

Bathing takes natural oils out of the skin, so do not do it too often. Always use dog shampoo or a human baby shampoo. Use water that is only just warm, not hot. Rinse the shampoo out thoroughly, otherwise the dog's skin will itch. Wet dogs

▼ **When bathing your dog, make sure that the water is lukewarm and that you do not get shampoo in his eyes.**

always shake themselves, so have a big towel ready. Keep the dog warm until it is dry.

Short coats, need to be brushed for a few minutes each day.
Medium coats, for example German Shepherds, normally need a daily brush and comb but extra time must be spent when the dog is moulting.
Wire-haired coats, need to be brushed and combed daily.

Wire-haired dogs need to go to a salon to be stripped when the coat is ready to be shed.
Long-haired coats, need lots of grooming. Watch for knots behind the ears. Remove tangles gently.
Woolly-haired coats, for example Poodles, need regular clipping and brushing and combing daily. Do not let hair grow down into the ears of these breeds, because it causes blockages.

11

TRAINING YOUR DOG

House training should begin as soon as you bring your new puppy home. Take the pup outside after every meal and praise it when it makes a mess or a puddle. If the dog makes a mess indoors, scold it and put it outside at once. Never rub your dog's nose in a puddle or mess. If the pup begins to circle or sniff, these are signs that it needs to go out. Young pups cannot wait all night, so put down lots of paper to catch accidents. Do not scold your pup for these.

Teach your dog its name as soon as possible. Also teach the dog to understand the word 'No' said in a sharp voice, but never hit a small puppy. Always use the same words as commands.

Teach 'Sit' by passing a titbit backwards high over the dog's head and saying 'Sit'. As the pup looks up it will begin to sit down. Push the bottom right down with your hand saying 'Sit' again and then give your pup lots of praise and the titbit.

Teach 'Down' by saying the word firmly, pointing at the floor and pushing behind the sitting puppy's shoulders.

To teach 'Stay', put the puppy's collar and lead on. Tell the dog to 'Sit' and 'Stay' and then step away, at the same time holding your hand out towards the dog with the palm facing it in a stopping signal. If the puppy moves, say 'No', put it back where it

▲ To fit a choke chain, place the chain over the dog's neck with the ring loop hanging down, as shown here.

◀ To teach your dog to come to you, first make him sit on a long lead. Give the command 'Come' and a gentle tug on the lead.

▼ A dog that strains hard on the lead is no fun to take for a walk. Basic training with a choke chain should cure this problem.

▼ A dog that does not want to keep up with you is as tiring as a dog that wants to surge ahead. Encourage the dog to walk by your side. Do not have a tug-of-war with him.

◄ When the dog is walking correctly to heel, the choke chain should hang loosely round his neck.

was and try again. When the dog does stay, walk back to it and give lots of praise. Mix your training sessions with lots of play periods.

Walking to heel can be taught when the puppy is happy to walk on the lead. If the puppy refuses to move, give lots of encouragement. Once your pup trots along happily on the lead, give a little tug and say 'Heel'. When the dog comes back beside you, give it lots of praise.

Do not use a choke chain on a young puppy. A large strong puppy could wear a leather or webbing choke collar.

▶ The Labrador Retriever loves to fetch things. He is especially good at retrieving from water.

THE HEALTHY DOG

◄ Borzois are dignified, gentle and quiet, but full of energy.

gets lost. Always keep your dog on the lead near traffic.

Health Check
To keep your dog healthy you must ensure it is inoculated, or injected, against diseases. Ask your vet for advice. Your dog must also be wormed regularly and checked for fleas, lice, ticks and ear mites. Below are listed some common dog illnesses and what to do about them.

Worms – a severe load of worms can kill a dog. Ask your vet for advice.
Fleas – these cause itching. They live in the carpet and

Exercise comes in many forms. It can be a game of throw and fetch in the garden or park, pavement walking, or a walk over fields in the countryside.

Exercise should be made interesting for the dog. Do not play the same game for too long, or take your dog along the same route each day. It is a good idea to allow your dog to mix with people and other dogs so that it learns how to behave in company.

When you take your dog out, make sure he is wearing a collar and tag in case he

▶ Your puppy's inoculations should be kept up to date.

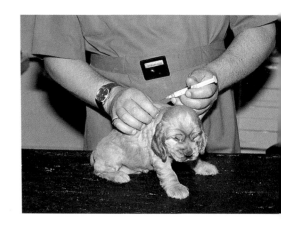

▼ If you are worried about any aspect of your dog's health, it is best to take him to the veterinarian for a check-up.

floor and only hop onto the dog to feed on its blood. Use flea powder or a spray.

Ticks – these parasites feed on the dog's blood. To remove, cover the tick with cold cooking oil, wait two minutes and twist it out in an anti-clockwise direction.

Ear Mites – these are greasy, dark brown smears in the ear. See your vet.

Lice – these look like little grains of sand and the skin

▶ A wet black nose is the classic sign of peak condition.

around them can be scabby. See your vet. Clean the dog's bedding.

Lameness – this can be caused by a thorn, cut, broken bone or torn ligament. See your vet.

Hip Dysplasia – this occurs in the joint of the hip. It can cause arthritis.

Cruciate Ligament – this is when the ligament that runs through the knee is stretched or broken.

Osteochondrosis – this is when a piece of cartilage breaks off inside a joint. It is very painful. See your vet.

Conjunctivitis – in this condition pus oozes from the eye. See your vet.

Progressive Retinal Atrophy – this eye condition can cause blindness.

DOG BREEDS

The many different breeds available are sorted into Groups. The Gundog Group contains sporting breeds like spaniels and retrievers. The Hound Group contains dogs as different as the compact Beagle and the lean, rangy Whippet. The Working Group (known as Herding Group in the USA) includes purposeful characters like Collies and St Bernards. The Terrier group comprises breeds like the Airedale and Westie. The Toy Group is made up of very small dogs like the Papillon and Yorkie. The last group is called the Utility Group (known as Non-sporting in the

▲ This cute-looking dog is a mongrel. They can make very good pets.

USA) and includes Bulldogs, Poodles and Schnauzers.

We have grouped the breeds here according to size, starting with small dogs and ending with extra-large ones.

SMALL DOGS

Papillon

The Papillon's large ears look like the wings of a butterfly when they are held erect. Its plumed tail is carried over its back and earned the dog the name 'Squirrel Spaniel'. The Papillon is an affectionate, intelligent dog who likes to romp. However he should be treated with kindness and not handled roughly.

Papillons must be groomed daily to keep their long, silky coat free of tangles. Papillons come in red, black or tricolour on a white ground. There is a drop-eared variety of this breed called the Phalene.

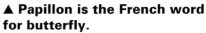

▲ Papillon is the French word for butterfly.

Yorkshire Terrier

This is a very lively toy terrier that may be too quick for elderly people and trip them up. Very small Yorkies are too delicate for families with small children. The Yorkie can be very noisy and needs a loving but firm owner. It can behave aggressively towards other dogs and this must be corrected.

Yorkies come in blue-grey and tan coat colours.

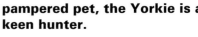

◀ Although very much a pampered pet, the Yorkie is a keen hunter.

▼ The Dachshunds shown here are all Miniatures. Top, Smooth-haired; middle, Long-haired; and, bottom, Wire-haired.

Dachshund

Dachshunds are brave dogs who make good companions. They can sometimes be quite naughty and need firm, loving owners. Although they are small, they have a deep bark and are alert. Dachshunds love to run about in the countryside as well as in town parks. They have very long backs and so must not be allowed to grow too fat as this will cause back trouble.

The Smooth-haired Dachshund needs very little grooming, but the Long-haired needs daily brushing and the Wire-haired's coat needs to be professionally stripped from time to time. The dog's ears should be checked regularly to make sure no grass seeds have entered into them.

Coat colours are rich red, black and tan, or any other colour except white.

Cavalier King Charles Spaniel

The charming little Cavalier King Charles has a sweet temper, an ever-wagging tail and is less noisy than many other small breeds. Its silky coat should never be trimmed and needs only a daily brushing to keep it clean.

Cavaliers have been popular lap dogs for about 400 years. They are named after King Charles II of England. Cavaliers are friendly if treated gently. They love to play and enjoy long walks although they do not need much exercise.

Cavalier colours are black and tan, ruby (solid red), tricolour and blenheim (red and white). Sadly, Cavaliers are prone to develop several health problems. Your puppy should be bought from a good breeder and be thoroughly examined by a vet before purchase. Do not buy a shy puppy. Cavaliers should be happy and brave.

Pug

Pugs are cheerful and amusing little dogs with short faces and chunky bodies. They make ideal pets for people of all ages as they are good-natured and friendly.

Pugs love to run about on a country walk or to stroll through the city streets on a lead. They soon settle to their new surroundings and are intelligent, good-humoured and easy to train.

The short coat of this breed does not need much grooming. However, you must be sure to check your pug's eyes regularly for injury.

The pug comes in two colours. These are fawn with a black mask or face, and jet black all over.

Do not allow your pug to become too fat as this may cause it to wheeze.

FACT FILE

Known at one time as the 'Comforter', the King Charles Spaniel is closely related to the Cavalier King Charles Spaniel. It is smaller than the Cavalier, with a shorter face and ears set lower on its head. The two breeds share the same coat colours of tan, ruby, tricolour and blenheim.

▼ **The sturdy appearance of the Pug belies his friendly, clownish character.**

▲ **Cavalier King Charles Spaniels have been popular since the seventeenth century.**

Shi Tzu

When Shi Tzu dogs were first brought to Europe, their sweet faces, long, silky hair and happy natures soon made them very popular.

Don't buy a Shi Tzu unless you enjoy grooming. The coat needs a lot of work, otherwise it will become matted and smelly and the dog will be very unhappy.

Shi Tzus are usually affectionate and playful dogs.

Any coat colour is allowed, but a white blaze on the forehead and a white tip to the tail are highly prized.

Your Shi Tzu will need a moderate amount of exercise and may enjoy chasing a ball. They love to play and will join in any fun with great enthusiasm. Because they have short noses and large eyes, Shi Tzus can suffer from eye injuries caused by scratches, so you must check your dog's eyes daily.

Cairn Terrier

The Cairn is hardy, cheerful and full of fire and courage. It was bred for hunting vermin among rocky areas and is

▲ The Cairn is a hardy dog which loves spending time outdoors.

ready to face anything and any weather in its harsh, wiry topcoat and thick, warm undercoat. Over-feeding on rich food can cause the Cairn to develop an itchy skin or even eczema.

The Cairn's coat needs to be stripped regularly to keep it in good condition. The dog

▼ A well groomed Shi Tzu looks delightful when its coat ripples with movement.

also needs daily brushing.

Cairns can behave aggressively towards other dogs and need firm training from puppyhood. They are intelligent dogs and often try to get their own way rather than obey orders.

Cairns are strong dogs who love exercise, so they should be kept fit and not allowed to grow fat. They will enjoy chasing a ball. This breed is usually healthy and lives into its teens. Some are good with children and some are snappy. They all need firm owners who will stand no nonsense. For such people they make really wonderful companions.

Coat colours are wheaten (fawn with a black face), brindle (brownish) and red.

Miniature Schnauzer

The Miniature Schnauzer is from the same basic stock as the Standard Schnauzer and shares his larger relative's love of the outdoors. He is equally at home, though, in the town. The Miniature is a sturdy little dog with a harsh, wiry coat, a beard and bushy eyebrows. It is intelligent and agile, and makes a faithful companion and family pet. Although it is small, it is tough enough to cope with energetic play and also steady enough to make a good pet for elderly people.

This dog must be groomed by stripping the coat regularly and its beard and whiskers must be kept clean to prevent them from becoming smelly. The coat and legs must be brushed daily. Do not allow your Schnauzer to become fat. This dog is a great athlete and must be kept fit.

The coat colours are solid black or pepper and salt, which is a mixture of grey, black and white.

▲ **A well tended Miniature Schnauzer will look very smart indeed.**

FACT FILE

• There are three types of Schnauzer : Miniature, Standard and Giant.
• The Standard Schnauzer was first bred in Germany some 500 years ago to herd farm animals. More recently the breed has been used as a guard dog.
• A Standard Schnauzer dog is about 5 in (12 cm) taller than a Miniature and about 7 in (17 cm) shorter than a Giant.

21

Shetland Sheepdog

This beautiful little dog looks like a miniature version of the Rough Collie (page 36). It has the same thick coat, half-pricked ears, long muzzle and history as a working sheepdog. Shelties are intelligent and easy to train.

The Sheltie's coat needs a lot of care, otherwise it will easily become matted. Ideally, the Sheltie should be groomed each day with a wide-toothed comb and a brush.

The breed is not suitable for harsh, noisy or bad-tempered people. It has a gentle, affectionate nature and needs quiet handling.

The coat colours are sable and white, tricolour or blue merle.

West Highland Terrier

This snow-white terrier is a hardy, courageous little dog, full of life and ready for anything. Despite their small size, Westies are very efficient house dogs. They have a strong desire to protect the people they love. This fearless, bold streak in the Westie's character shows too in the dog's love of play. Westies certainly do not need pampering. Instead, they need lots of exercise. Chasing a ball is a favourite game, even though they may not always want to give it back! Like most intelligent dogs, Westies will try to get their own way and need to be gently reminded that they are not the boss. Westies can be aggressive towards other dogs, and need firm handling.

The coat must be kept clean and well groomed. It will need regular stripping.

▲ Shetland Sheepdogs should be happy, friendly dogs. Do not buy a shy puppy.

Corgi

Corgis are very courageous, calm and fearless and are good workers. They learn quickly and like to be kept busy. Most Corgis are good-tempered, but they will not stand teasing.

FACT FILE

- Blue merle Shetland Sheepdogs often have blue eyes. They can be found with one blue and one brown eye.
- The West Highland White has very strong jaws because of its history as a rat catcher.
- Corgis were once known as 'heelers' because they used to drive cattle by nipping at their heels.

◀ **West Highland Terriers are tough yet exuberant little dogs.**

▼ **The Corgi tends to enjoy playing with other dogs rather than people.**

Well-trained Corgis do well in obedience trials and make excellent retrievers. Their short legs and heavy bodies make agility tests difficult.

Corgis have short, thick coats to keep out the cold. The coat should be brushed every day and combed thoroughly while the dog is moulting. Coat colours are red, sable, fawn, black or tan, all with a white trim.

Corgis have few health problems and usually live to a good age. Do not let your Corgi become too fat as this will cause heart or breathing problems and make the dog bad-tempered.

MEDIUM DOGS

Schnauzer

Schnauzers are playful and tolerant when young, and should get on well with all the family. Adult dogs are good-natured and careful, and become extremely attached to those they know well.

They learn quickly and are good at competition work, especially agility trials. The dog needs plenty of exercise and must not be allowed to become fat. Ball games will give it both fun and exercise.

The Schnauzer's rough, wiry coat must be groomed often and stripped regularly to keep it smart. Its bushy eyebrows, beard and legs must be kept well brushed.

There are two coat colours. These are solid black and pepper and salt, which is a mixture of grey, black and white.

Whippet

The Whippet gives the appearance of being a nervous, shivering, timid breed, but it is actually very calm and confident.

Whippets are very agile and good jumpers. Training is easy, but don't expect your Whippet to score top marks in obedience trials – they are simply not interested in such competitions.

◀ **Schnauzers need plenty of exercise. They enjoy ball games.**

▼ **Whippets are graceful dogs.**

exercise. The breed comes in many coat colours.

The Whippet has no serious health problems and is one of the hardiest breeds there is.

Basset Hound

The Basset is easy-going and affectionate, but beware! if the dog sniffs an interesting smell while out on a walk, off it will go.

Their short, sleek coats need little care, but their ears must be checked often for mites or infections. Coat colours are tricolour, lemon and white or tan and white.

Bassets should never be fed on dry foods as these can cause bloat, a serious stomach condition which can even cause death.

The breed has a short, sleek, easily cared-for coat, is very clean and has a sweet, gentle nature. Whippets fit well into almost any home, provided it is not cold or damp and they get enough

▲▼ **Basset Hounds need a lot of exercise to make sure they do not become fat.**

FACT FILE
• The Standard Schnauzer is an ancient German breed that has been used as a vermin-killer and a guard dog.
• The Basset came to Britain from France in 1872.
• The Whippet looks like a miniature Greyhound, but the breeds are not closely related.

◄ **The Border Collie loves to herd sheep.**

Border Collie

Until a few years ago no one minded what this breed looked like as long as it did its traditional job of sheep herding well. But nowadays breeders are trying to make the dogs look more similar.

Border Collies need to work and to be kept busy and for this reason they do not always make good pets. If they get bored they will develop irritating habits, like racing up and down, barking. They are not suitable dogs for owners who are out all day and who will not give them plenty of exercise regularly.

The coat must be brushed daily to remove tangles. The feet and ears must also be checked for injuries.

Coat colours are black, white, liver, brown, merle and tricolour.

► **The Bearded Collie gets its name from its long beard.**

Bearded Collie

Bearded Collies are active, intelligent, gentle dogs who love to please their owners. They are much softer temperamentally than other breeds of their kind and make better pets as a result.

Only choose a Bearded Collie if you like grooming! The dog's coat is extremely thick and needs to be groomed thoroughly every day to remove knots and tangles.

Bearded Collies are easily trained and active enough to take part in many dog sports and competitions. They make good companions for active, outdoor people. The coat colours are slate-grey, black

and brown, all with a white trim which makes the coat attractive.

Some Bearded Collies suffer from eye and hip problems.

Beagle

Beagles have an excellent sense of smell and have been used as hunting dogs for over 500 years.

The Beagle is an active, cheerful dog with a kind, easy-going nature. It has great stamina and can run for miles. These dogs do need a lot of exercise, so bear this in mind. Beagles are generally very good-tempered and are not aggressive towards other dogs. This is probably because they were bred as pack dogs, and even today's beagles seem happiest when they are in a group with their fellows.

Beagles are not always easy to train as single pets, so owners need to have patience and determination. However, Beagles are also very playful and can become very attached to their owners. They do have one annoying habit – they tend to run off after any interesting scent. Firm training during puppyhood should correct this.

The coat is usually very smart and glossy. It can be any colour except liver and white. Only a little grooming is required because the coat is so short.

They are usually healthy and tend to live to a good age. Check the dog's ears daily for grass seeds or mites.

▲▼ Beagles are very bouncy and active and are among the most popular of the Hound Group of dogs.

27

Norwegian Buhund

This attractive and hardy dog has been used for hundreds of years in Norway as a guard dog. Some Buhunds can be too noisy and need to be trained well.

Buhunds make good pets for active, outdoor people. They can be quite playful and need lots of exercise. They will accept training if you are firm and kind and, above all, determined.

The dog's thick, coarse coat needs grooming daily and thorough combing when the dog is moulting. The coat colours are fawn, light red, sable and black.

▼ The Norwegian Buhund is fearless, brave and cheerful.

English Cocker Spaniel

The breed's high-domed head, low-hanging ears, sad eyes, sturdy body and silky coat make it a very attractive show dog. Working Cocker Spaniels are less beautiful than their showbiz relatives, but are fast and obedient and much better workers. Both types of Cocker should be active and willing to please. They are good with people of all ages.

◄ English Cockers were bred to hunt birds called woodcocks.

Cockers must be groomed daily and should have their ears checked for mites. At the first sign of ear trouble you must take your dog to the vet. The coat needs to be stripped by hand. Coat colours are tricolour, red roan, blue roan and black and red.

The coat of a show dog takes a great deal of care. Pet dogs usually have their coats clipped shorter than show dogs and this makes grooming easier. You must check carefully for ear mites.

American Cockers learn quickly and are willing to please. They could be trained for competition work provided their training is done kindly.

There are many coat colours. This breed can suffer from serious eye problems and it is advisable to make sure that the parents of your puppy are free of such troubles.

American Cocker Spaniel

This is a most attractive dog. It has dark, seal-like eyes, low-set, feathered ears and heavy fringes on its coat. The American Cocker is sweet-natured, happy and obedient. Its ears are especially sensitive and should not be pulled or handled roughly.

FACT FILE

• Norwegian Buhunds belong to a group of breeds called Spitz dogs. Many Spitz dogs come from the countries that make up Scandinavia. Spitz dogs have thick coats, pointed ears and noses, and all have curled-up tails.
• American Cocker Spaniels are smaller than English Cockers because the birds they are required to retrieve in the USA are smaller. Quail, a favourite US game bird, is virtually unknown in Britain.

▼ **American Cocker Spaniels (top) are smaller than English Cockers by about 2 in (5 cm) and proportionately less heavy.**

Welsh Springer Spaniel

The Welsh Springer is lighter in build than the English Springer, its ears do not carry so much feathering of hair, and the coat is easier to care for. However, like its English cousin, the Welsh Springer must be brushed every day. The legs and underbelly need special attention as these areas are most likely to pick up debris.

Welsh Springers are very playful and generally good-tempered. Training must be firm but never harsh.

Coat colours are rich red and white. The breed may suffer from eye and hip problems.

English Springer Spaniel

There are two types of English Springer. The working dog is very fast and active and loves to be busy. It will get into mischief if it becomes bored. It is not as handsome as the show Springer which is also calmer and bigger.

Springers are intelligent and easy to train. They make good competition dogs for obedience trials and are good with people of all ages. Like all working dogs, Springers need firm discipline.

Springers need lots of exercise. They must be groomed daily and their ears checked for mites. The hair between their toes should be trimmed from time to time. Coat colours are liver and white, black and white or tricolour and white.

Springers may suffer from eye and hip problems.

▼ English (top) and Welsh Springer Spaniels (bottom) are very active, outdoor dogs.

FACT FILE

- The energetic and busy English Springer Spaniel works further and faster than any other type of spaniel.
- An old Irish name for the Irish Water Spaniel was 'the rat-tailed dog with the cow-dung eyes'. This is not very flattering, but these dogs are usually much loved by their owners.

are intelligent, sensible and calm dogs. They do need lots of exercise. The breed is very agile, too, so your garden needs to be well fenced.

The coat will become quite smelly if it is not groomed often. Sometimes bald areas appear around the eyes. If this happens, carefully smear a little petroleum jelly round the area to encourage the hair to grow.

The coat is always a deep, rich chocolate-brown. Some dogs have hip dysplasia.

▼ **Water Spaniels - Irish (top); American (below).**

Water Spaniels

▲ **The Welsh Springer Spaniel is an excellent hunter in all seasons.**

The Irish Water Spaniel is an ancient breed of gundog. The American Water Spaniel, thought to be a development of the Irish type, has the same chocolate-brown curly coat and strong build. He is smaller by about 2 in (5 cm). The main difference between the two is in the head (the American Water Spaniel has no topknot) and in the tail, which is plumed rather than partly bare.

Water Spaniels are good-tempered dogs and will work in all weathers. Training should be easy, because they

31

Bulldog

The modern Bulldog looks really fierce, with its massive head and short, thick body that is wide at the front end and narrow at the hips. In truth the Bulldog is kind-hearted, brave and a very sensible dog. It makes a wonderful and endearing pet for the whole family.

The Bulldog is not a very energetic animal and does not need much exercise, especially in hot weather. It does need loving owners, a warm home and a soft bed. Bulldogs are seldom aggressive towards people. However, they do need firm training to teach them good

▼ **The fierce-looking Bulldog has a lovely nature.**

▶ **German Spitzes can be excitable.**

manners towards other dogs.

The breed does not need much grooming, but the creases in the skin around the face must be kept clean. Bulldogs have very short noses and this can make their breathing wheezy.

Coat colours are red, fawn, smust, pied, brindle and white. Bulldogs suffer from many health problems and you would be wise to take out veterinary insurance.

German Spitz

The German Spitz comes in three sizes called Klein (small), Mittel (medium) and Grosse (large).

The Spitz is a happy, active, playful dog, affectionate and a good companion. It moves very quickly, though and may cause old people to trip up. The breed tends to be excitable and this can cause them to make mistakes during competitions.

Spitzes have excellent hearing and a large streak of self-preservation. If a stranger enters your property, the dog will stand at a safe distance and bark non-stop.

Staffies can be aggressive towards other animals, so start training your puppy when it is very young.

This breed can be very excitable, so they need plenty of exercise to use up their energy. They are not very suitable for obedience work and sometimes sulk.

The Staffie's short, sleek coat needs very little grooming. There are many different coat colours. Staffies are very hardy dogs.

They can become too noisy, however, and must be trained to be quiet on command.

Because of its fluffed-out topcoat and thick, warm undercoat, this breed does not feel the cold and can live in a kennel out of doors. There are many coat colours. Spitzes are healthy dogs and usually live to a good age.

Staffordshire Bull Terrier

Staffies like long, energetic walks, ball games and tug o' war, but if the weather turns cold and damp they would much rather snuggle up by the fire.

▶ **Staffordshire Bull Terriers love to be comfortable.**

33

LARGE DOGS

Greyhound

This is one of the oldest of all the dog breeds. It has been used for hundreds of years to catch prey like rabbits for people to eat.

As you can imagine, the breed needs a lot of exercise. A long gallop in the fields and some road walking each day will keep the Greyhound fit. Many ex-racing dogs need a good home and usually make fine companions. They are quiet and very gentle with people. However, ex-racers do need to be retrained so that they will not chase cats and small dogs.

Greyhounds are easy to train as pets, but they are not very good at competition work. Their coats are easy to care for and come in many different colours. Greyhounds are very healthy and live for many years.

Standard Poodle

The largest member of the Poodle family is tough, intelligent and a good working dog. It will retrieve game from land or water, is good at scenting and agility work and is a natural show-off. Standard Poodles need lots of exercise.

Pet or working Poodles usually have their coats clipped short all over in a puppy or lamb clip. This type of coat needs to be brushed and combed each day to prevent matting. Poodles'

▼ Greyhounds make affectionate family pets.

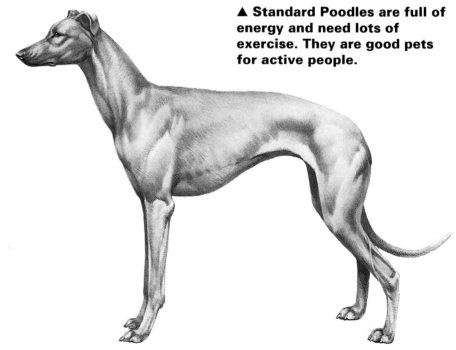

▲ Standard Poodles are full of energy and need lots of exercise. They are good pets for active people.

34

◀ **Greyhounds do very well in the show ring. They move well and need little preparation.**

coats are made of wool not fur and do not moult, so these dogs are ideal for people with allergies.

The coat colours are solid white, blue-grey, apricot, black and chocolate. Poodles suffer from eye problems. They also sometimes suffer from skin allergies.

Airedale Terrier

Airedales are brave dogs. They are also affectionate and good-natured.

To get the best out of an Airedale, you need to be firm and active. These dogs need plenty of exercise. They like a good gallop and brisk road walking, and will enjoy a game of tug. Airedales can be aggressive towards other dogs and this must be corrected in early puppyhood.

The breed can do well in competition and agility work but will sulk if they become bored. They are excellent guard dogs.

The harsh coat must be brushed daily to prevent it from matting and becoming smelly. The hair does not moult. The coat colour is rich tan with a black saddle.

▲ **A good daily gallop, some brisk road walking, as well as tugging games in the garden, will keep the Airedale fit.**

white, tricolour, blue merle and white body with sable, tricolour or blue merle heads. This breed sometimes suffers from hip and eye problems.

German Shepherd

German Shepherds are handsome and intelligent. They are active and need to be kept busy. If they are left alone or become bored they may whine endlessly. Well-trained, well-bred German Shepherds make good pets, but shy, nervous dogs are not to be trusted.

The coat must be groomed each day and needs extra attention when the dog is moulting. Coat colours vary.

German Shepherds can suffer from hip dysplasia.

Rottweiler

Rottweilers are brave, intelligent dogs with kindly natures. However, an over-excited Rottweiler can be very dangerous, so proper training is vital. Male Rottweilers can be aggressive towards other dogs. Good training at an early age will correct this.

Rough Collie

This breed was once used to herd sheep but it is now kept mainly as a companion and show dog. It has won many awards at Crufts Dog Show.

Rough Collies are very affectionate with their family and friends but aloof with strangers. Sometimes they are quiet and dignified; at other times they like to play. They are intelligent and good with people of all ages and are not usually aggressive. However, they are very sensitive to pain, nor do they like being teased. The thick coat needs a good brushing each day and very thorough grooming when the dog is moulting. Rough Collies love exercise and should have a good run and some road walking each day to keep their muscles strong.

Coat colours are sable and

FACT FILE

- Rottweilers are a German breed. They were known in Roman times when they were used to herd cattle and pull small carts.
- Like all big, powerful dogs, Rottweilers can be dangerous if they are not properly trained from puppyhood. In recent years there has been a problem with bad breeding and bad ownership. Some Rottweilers have been bred from unsuitable parents to satisfy demand. Dogs have also been bought by people who have not trained them.

▼ **A well-bred well-trained Rottweiler is trustworthy and good with all the family.**

▲ **German Shepherds should be happy and self-confident.**

Despite their large size, Rottweilers are very agile and seem to enjoy all kinds of competition work. Rottweilers have large appetites, but must not be allowed to get fat. The dog needs quite a lot of exercise and very little grooming.

The coat colour is always black and tan. Rottweilers have problems with eyelids that turn inwards, their ligaments and hip dysplasia.

DOG BREEDS

Golden Retriever

Golden Retrievers are kindly, affectionate, intelligent and easy to train. They are not usually aggressive towards other dogs and are much too friendly to make convincing guard dogs.

Goldens need lots of exercise and love to gallop across the fields. They do

▲ Golden Retrievers are very well-mannered dogs, even in a group.

well in competition work.

The coat ideally needs to be brushed and combed every day to avoid tangles. Dogs moult once a year and bitches twice a year.

Coat colours are shades of golden to cream, but not deep red or mahogany. The breed suffers from eye problems and hip dysplasia.

▼ Golden Retrievers (top) and Labradors (below) are excellent gundogs.

Labrador

This excellent gundog has been used for many purposes. It has a short, waterproof coat that allows it to retrieve game, including fish, from cold water. The Labrador is intelligent and eager to please. It is used as a guide dog for the blind and as a sniffer dog by the police and armed forces.

The breed usually does well in shows and also makes an excellent companion and family dog. Labradors are very good with small children. They will bark if a stranger approaches, but are not very good guard dogs as they are too kindly. In spite of this, they must be trained properly to be completely obedient and they need lots of exercise to prevent boredom, otherwise they may go off alone and get into trouble. Labradors love games of throw-and-fetch and all competition work.

The coat needs only a little grooming and comes in black, yellow and liver. This breed suffers from eye problems and hip dysplasia.

Dalmatian

This dog is often referred to as the Plum Pudding Dog because of its spotty coat.

Dalmatians are not always easy to train and do not seem as eager to please as certain other dog breeds. They are mostly kept as elegant, good-natured family pets.

Dalmatians are active and have great stamina. They need lots of exercise.

The short coat needs little grooming. It is completely white when the puppies are born. The spots, which should be even and round, appear later. They are either black or liver-coloured on a pure white background.

▼ **The Dalmatian's coat is very striking and the dog is a favourite at shows.**

FACT FILE
• The Dalmatian takes its name from a region of Yugoslavia, where the breed is said to have originated. The dog was bred to accompany fashionable people.
• Cartoon Dalmatians were the popular stars of the exciting and funny Walt Disney film called A Hundred and One Dalmatians.

▲ **The Irish Setter has a good temperament.**

Irish Setter

This beautiful gundog has a silky, deep red, long-feathered coat, lovely eyes and slim muscular build. In recent years Irish Setters have been bred more for the show ring and they have lost many of the qualities needed in working dogs.

Irish Setters are kindly and affectionate towards people and other animals, but they are not easy to train.

Irish Setters need a great deal of exercise and tend to be quite thin. They are not big eaters and are sometimes very choosy about their food. The fine, glossy coat must be groomed daily to keep it shiny and free of tangles. The only coat colour is a rich, deep red.

Some Irish Setters suffer from an eye problem called night blindness.

Borzoi

This ancient Russian breed of wolfhound is dignified, gentle and quiet, but also full of energy. Borzois love to gallop and need a good run each day, as well as some walking on a lead. They are not usually aggressive and do not make good guard dogs.

Borzois make excellent show dogs, but are not good obedience trial or competition dogs, although they are easy enough to train as pets. The coat is quite easy to keep clean, but will need a good daily brushing to prevent tangles from forming. The coat colour varies.

▲ **Old English Sheepdogs have very thick coats and feel the heat in summer.**

▼ **The Borzoi is a noble and dignified dog that loves to gallop.**

Old English Sheepdog

This popular breed is also called the Bobtail. It is descended from an ancient herding dog once used by shepherds. The coat colours of this early breed were brown and white. Today's Old English Sheepdog has a grey, grizzled or blue coat with a white trim.

The thick, shaggy topcoat and dense undercoat of this dog is very difficult to keep tidy. If the dog is not groomed thoroughly every day the hair will become very matted.

The breed is usually kind and intelligent. Make sure you buy from a good breeder who will not sell you a puppy from bad-tempered parents

Old English Sheepdogs love exercise and competition work and are easily trained.

The breed suffers from hip dysplasia and eye problems.

FACT FILE
The Old English Sheepdog has been a popular breed at dog shows for many years. People often applaud when he enters the ring. Breeders have encouraged the coat to become thick and long to enhance the dog's looks.

FACT FILE

- The Bernese Mountain Dog is named after the Canton of Berne, in Switzerland, where it comes from.
- The Giant Schnauzer is descended from the old cattle dogs of south Germany, but some people think that it is related to the Great Dane. It was first shown in Munich in 1909 under the name 'Russian Bear Schnauzer'.
- The famous American Helen Keller was the first person to bring the Akita into the United States. She was given a puppy as a present by an official in Akita in 1937.

Bernese Mountain Dog

This dog is descended from ancient herding dogs used by the Romans.

These are kindly, easy-going dogs that get on well with people of all ages. This is not altogether surprising because although the Bernese is known as a working dog, he always lived as a member of the family and became a pet as well as a worker.

The Bernese needs quite a lot of exercise. It is a highly intelligent dog and easily trained.

The coat should be brushed each day. It is very attractive, soft and silky, and gleams when brushed. When the dog is moulting, the coat needs a thorough combing too.

The coat colour is tricolour. Some Bernese suffer from hip dysplasia.

Giant Schnauzer

This is the largest of the three Schnauzer types. The other types are the Miniature (see page 21) and the Standard Schnauzers (see page 24).

The Giant Schnauzer is an excellent working dog, strong and reliable. It makes a good guard dog, or companion and family dog. The Schnauzer is sensible and kind with its family and friends. It has a big heart and is seldom nasty.

The Schnauzer is an active dog that loves to work but is also playful and boisterous. It needs to belong to an active owner and also to be trained firmly from an early age in order to learn good manners. This dog loves to run and needs plenty of exercise.

The coat colours are black or pepper and salt. The coat is harsh, wiry and waterproof and needs to be stripped regularly. The dog's bushy

▼ **In its Swiss homeland the Bernese Mountain Dog has been used to pull small milk carts.**

The breed is noted for its faithfulness to its family and strong sense of loyalty. It is very affectionate and loves human company.

Akitas are very strong dogs and need responsible owners. They may be too strong for young children or elderly people. Training should be very firm. They enjoy plenty of exercise and seldom bark unless a stranger approaches their owner's property.

There are numerous coat colours, but no more than one third of the coat should be white. Some Akitas suffer from hip dysplasia.

◄ **Giant Schnauzers are full of fun yet sensible.**

▼ **Akitas make good guard dogs and family pets.**

eyebrows and whiskers must be kept well brushed.

Schnauzers are usually healthy but you should check that your puppy's parents do not have hip dysplasia.

Akita

The Akita comes from the Japanese island of Honshu where it was used as a guard dog and for hunting. It was brought to the USA after World War II by returning American servicemen, but did not become popular for quite some time. Today it can be seen in show rings all over the world.

The breed belongs to the Spitz group of dogs and is very tough and hardy. Akitas are intelligent and can be used in obedience and agility work. Most make good companions and guard dogs.

GIANT DOGS

◄ **The St Bernard needs a lot of food and water to keep its massive frame sturdy and healthy.**

Saint Bernard

The Saint Bernard is a handsome, gentle, obedient dog that needs less exercise than you might think.

Training should be quite easy as these dogs are very willing to please. They are not noisy. Saint Bernards do dribble quite a lot, which some people do not like. Their coats need a great deal of grooming.

Coat colours are orange, mahogany-brindle or red-brindle, all with white. St Bernards have problems with hip dysplasia and hanging eyelids.

Great Dane

Dogs of this type were used for boar hunting in the Middle Ages. Today's Great Dane is a tall, noble dog. It can be trained to do well in competition work.

If you buy a puppy from a breeder, make sure that the mother is not very thin and that she is not nervous or shy.

Too much exercise can strain the heart of a Great Dane, but they do need to be kept busy and to mix with people and other dogs. The short coat does not need much grooming. Coat colours are fawn, black, brindle, blue and harlequin, which is a white background with oddly shaped coloured patches on it.

Great Danes need soft beds to avoid getting sore patches on their elbows.

Newfoundland

The Newfoundland is a good-natured, calm and even-tempered breed. However, puppies need firm but kind handling to teach them good manners.

The Newfoundland's heavy, oily coat needs a thorough brushing each day to remove tangles and keep the coat clean and glossy. These dogs do not need a great deal of

▼ **The Great Dane is a tall, elegantly built dog.**

▲ **Newfoundlands are water dogs.**

exercise, but should be walked every day. The coat colour is always black.

The breed suffers from hip dysplasia. Puppies will develop a bone disease called rickets if their diet does not contain enough calcium.

FACT FILE

The most famous Saint Bernard in history was called Barry, who saved over forty travellers in the Alps during the nineteenth century. Sadly, one day he was mistaken for a wolf, and shot.

INDEX

PHOTOGRAPH CREDITS

The publishers would like to thank Marc Henrie for supplying the majority
of the photographs reproduced in this book. Thanks also to Sally Ann Thompson/
Animal Photography for the photographs on pages 19, 34, 43 and 44; Frank Lane
Picture Agency page 7; and the Bridgeman Art Library page 6 (right).